Is My Little Boy Blue?

Copyright© 2020 Gail Holmes

All rights reserved. No part of this book may be reproduced in any manner whatsoever without written permission except in the case of brief quotations embodied in critical articles and reviews.

ISBN:9780988777583

Written by Gail Holmes
IsMyLittleBoyBlue@gmail.com

Illustrated by Bradley Jenkins
bradley.jenkins0@gmail.com

All content found in this book (including text, images, or other formats) were created for entertainment purposes only. The content is not intended to be a substitute for professional medical advice, diagnosis, or treatment. Always seek the advice of your physician or other qualified health provider with any questions you may have regarding a medical condition. Never disregard professional medical advice or delay in seeking it because of something you have read in this book. If you think you may have a medical emergency, call your doctor, go to the emergency department, or call 911 immediately. This book does not recommend or endorse any specific treatments, tests, physicians, products, procedures, opinions, or other information that may be mentioned in the story. Reliance on any information in this book is solely at your own risk. The opinions and views expressed in this book have no relation to those of any academic, hospital, health practice or other institution. The book, author, publisher, and printer assume no responsibility for how you use the content in this book. You are responsible for your own health and safety at all times, and you are responsible for the health and safety of your dependents. This book is not intended to diagnose, treat, cure, or prevent any disease.

Once upon a time, there was a courageous, brilliant boy full of adventure.

He loved books and animals.
His favorite thing to eat was chicken.

His name was Michael.
He had beautiful brown eyes and big curls atop his head.

**Michael was special.
He told funny jokes and wrote wonderful stories.**

Everyone loved him, and he loved his friends, but sometimes he could not sit with them at lunch because the sight and smells of their foods made him sick.

Sometimes he did not want to play with his friends because he wanted to be all alone.

One day, Michael's mom asked him, "Is my little boy blue?"
Michael looked at his mom, curiously, "What? Of course, I'm not blue."
"No," his mom said, "Not your color, your mood. Are you sad?"

Michael looked at his mom, his big beautiful eyes watered, and one single tear fell.
"Yes, Mommy. I'm sad. I'm sad most of the time."

Michael's mom kissed and hugged him real tight.
She wished hugs and kisses could make him better.
But she knew, just as she couldn't hug and kiss away Michael's ear infections or the flu, that she could not love away his sadness.

So off to the doctor they went.

Michael met a nice doctor, a psychiatrist. The doctor put Michael at ease.
She explained that depression caused his sadness, that Michael did not cause his illness, and that he was not alone.
The doctor said, "Other children have depression, and I am very proud of you for coming to my office to talk about your feelings."

The doctor explained, "Sometimes when you are ill, you can get better by changing your diet or exercise routine. Maybe talking with others can take away your sadness.
But sometimes, like when you have an ear infection or the flu, medicine makes you feel better."

After taking his medicine, there were more bright colors in Michael's world. He saw rainbows where once there were only gray skies.

His medicine was not a magic pill, but because he was courageous and talked about his feelings, Michael could say, "Every day is not happy, but I am happier than I was before. I am Little Boy Blue no more!"

Milton Keynes UK
Ingram Content Group UK Ltd.
UKHW050154181123
432799UK00003B/33